Google SEO Marketing Book - Offpage SEO For Business, Social Bookmarking N Backlinks

Google SEO
Optimization For Business
(Facebook ,Google Plus ,Twitter
SEO Techniques)

By Sanjana Koul

Published by:

Sanjana Koul

© Copyright 2015 – Sanjana Koul

ISBN-13: 978-1507824559

ISBN-10: 1507824556

Table of Contents

Contents

Chapter 1:
What Is SEO?

Search Engine Optimization abbreviated as SEO is considered as the major aspect in increasing the traffic of one's own website. The concept behind good SEO is no longer a secret. SEO are techniques which are used to make your web site "Search engine" friendly and increases probability of placing your website among high ranks in searches.SEO is considered as the most beneficial method among all the driving leads as the leads you get from SEO are free. You can never achieve best results from SEO overnight.

Black Hat V/S White Hat

The Black and White hats are two opposite terms with respect to search engine optimization. Black hat is the method in which you can fool the search engine and can get high traffic to your website but with this method there are more chances of your website getting banned with the change in search engine algorithm. On the contrary white hat is the technique in which you can expect long term traffic to your website as there is no acceptance of "fooling" term and hence the traffic which you get for your website is genuine and long term also. White SEO is also termed as "ethical" and "correct" SEO's.

BEWARE..!!

You can get unlimited benefit from SEO. You just need to be updated with new SEO tools and software. Always spent certain amount of time in research before buying any SEO software as the search engine algorithms are being changed continuously. Now the question arises here as why search engine needs to change their algorithm?? The answer is simple to avoid high traffic on a particular website through technique like "black hat". Thus change in algorithm of search engine helps users to get data relevant to their searches. There are various types of Search Engine Optimization (SEO) tools for Yahoo, MSN and Google. It is difficult to crack search engine algorithm but with the use of proper SEO tools you can make it and hence promoting your website becomes quite easy.

Meaning of good SEO Content

The quality and helpful information that you provide to users through either website or blogs are considered as good SEO content. The main factor upon which the "good content" depends upon is the content of your competing websites. The content that you will be using in your website should be unique so that it can pass the duplicate content filters. Therefore it is mandatory to index your content article before you submit it to any search engine. The "new" search engine algorithm can trace your content and can see who has published it first so u should be sure that you have put your content on website or blog first before you submit it to article directories.

Chapter2:
What Is Offpage SEO?

Offpage SEO is a technique that can be helpful in improving the rank of search engine but this is done off your site. By offsite I mean the promotion of your website or blog is not done on your own site but can be made possible with the help of other sites. Offpage optimization with Google has become more important as it pays more attention to the relevant links.

For Offpage SEO you have to pay attention to:

- The number of links which is connected to your website.

- The more the link, the more the beneficial it will be for you.The type of site which is connected to your site should be quite relevant to your site else it is of no use and the search engine has also the power to backlist such sites.

- Use of "anchor text" is also helpful for Offpage SEO. Anchor text is a text which is liked to your website for getting more information on that text. Here also the case is same the "text" should be relevant to your "site".

What Are Backlinks?

BACKLINK is considered as a link which is connected to your website through other websites. Backlink is a strategy that will increase your chance to be on the first page of "GOOGLE" search engine. When you provide link of your site on other website the readers can easily visit to your site by just clicking on that particular link. Google keep record of such links and observe it and take it as a signal that you have gained authority in that particular topic and hence can help you in ranking high if a search is made on that topic.

In simple words Backlinks are considered as hyperlinks which directs to the URL (Universe Resource Locator) address of your website, articles or blogs.

Let me explain backlink with an example:

Let's say website 1 has a link on the main page that re-directs to website 2.Now website 2 has one Backlink from website 1.How this will be useful for website 2??

The person reading website1 will click on your link (if found interesting) for more information hence increasing traffic to your website and which results in good page rank.

Why Backlinks Are Needed?

There are following two reasons for it:

- **Direct traffic:**If user will find the topic interesting he can click on your Backlink for further more information. Make sure you are providing relevant information and you are not disappointing the user.
- **Search Engine Traffic:**If you have more Backlinks that redirects to your website, blogs or articles it can be better for your page and can help for good ranking in search engine results.

Where Should I Place My Backlink?

Placement of Backlink depends upon following two factors:

- **Subject matter:**Placing a Backlink on a site which is not related to your site will not matter that much. For example if u have a page on kitchen ware there is no point if you will place its link on gardening site. It's obvious the user who will be interested in reading about gardening will not go to your link as it is nowhere related to gardening.

- **Quality of the site:**The quality of the site will obviously matter. If you are providing Backlink on a page that isn't well-reputed then it won't affect that much to your site. This is because the backlinked site itself isn't that much impressive for the users. For example if you will provide Backlink to your website on a popular site with high PR like ezinearticles, that will count more for your website rather than providing it on any other site with low PR.

Do Bad Backlinks Exist?

No there is nothing like bad Backlink but you should keep in mind following two points:

- There are sites that are of no value or have little importance and placing a backlink on such website can be related to your website traffic as no traffic or quite little traffic respectively.

- There are also sites which are banned or possess illegal material. Such sites also won't help that much for the rank of your page.

NOTE: You can try to leave backlink on a "related" site of low quality with the faith that someday that low quality site will increase its quality and hence which will result in good traffic to your website

Chapter 3:
DO Follow V/S No Follow Links

Do Follow Link

A hyperlink with the help of which Google, yahoo, Bing and many other search engine follows the link are called Do follow link. This is the definition of "Do follow link". Let me explain you in detail.To get a good rank in Google you need to have a number of backlinks that will be pointing to your site and search engine considers only those links that can be followed and is a "Do follow" link. More Do Follow links will be pointing to your site more traffic you will get for your site which results in good rank in SERP (Search Engine Result Page).

No Follow Link

A hyperlink which will not allow Google, yahoo, Bing and many other search engines to follow the link are called "No follow" link.

Use Of No Follow Link

The use of "No follow" link is to avoid the spam comments in the blog.So if you do not want any user to get the benefit from your website or blog you can make use of "No follow" links. Wordpress and Blogger, by default, have "No follow" link for comments in order to avoid spam comments.

Determine Whether Link Is "Do Follow" Or "No Follow"

Right click on that particular page that you want to check

- Go to "view page source" option.
- Press Ctrl+F and do the search for "nofollow".

Important Terms

(a) Inbound links

The link that points to your website through other website or webpage are called Inbound links.

(b) Outbound links

The link that points to external website through your website are called outbound links.

(c) Internal links

The links which points to other pages that lies within your website are known as internal links.

Chapter 4:
Offpage SEO Techniques

Social Media

Social Marketing is known all over the world these days. You just need to sign up for very popular sites like Google+, Facebook, Twitter etc and make your own profile in these sites. It will help you to widen your contacts throughout the world. More the contacts more the possibility of sharing your page, article, website, blogs etc. The more the sharing the great will be the online reputation of a particular page, article, website, blog etc.

Now how can you build online reputation through social media like Facebook, Twitter and Google+ is explained below in detail

(a) Facebook

Creating a "FANPAGE" on Facebook is one of the great way to make your website known in a "FACEBOOK" site. Now what is "FANPAGE"??

A Fanpage is a Facebook Page where you can notify people about your company and everything related to it which includes promotions, new blog entries, upcoming events, competitions etc. If you will get a "LIKE" on this page then the user who liked the page will become the "FAN" of your page.

It is quite easy to create your own page on a Facebook. Many companies do that but making the "FANPAGE" worth will be possible only if it is utilized properly. Only a good Fan page can help you in increasing the traffic for your website and hence helping in growing your business.

If you will go through the following six steps you will be able to make a profitable Facebook Fanpage.

Advertisement through profile image:

Now when you see any page the very first thing that you will notice about that page will be the profile image so make sure that you are uploading a good profile image to attract users. The profile image can be the logo of your company or any good picture of the company. Only the best marketers can make out that the profile image can speak a lot about your page.

One more useful trick that you can utilize for profile image is by keeping the image which will have a arrow pointed towards the "LIKE" button of your page and many other useful tricks like this you can apply for an "attractive" profile image.

Facebook-Thumbnails:

Like profile picture, thumbnail can also display valuable information. At the start of every Facebook page you can have five recent thumbnail images. Now the public uses thumbnail images for displaying images of their recent night outs or pubs. But for a professional use these thumbnail images can be used in a more valuable way. You can put the images of your products that you are selling, you can also put the links to any social networking site which will have your website, you can also display images of clients with whom you have worked and can also add a short description with it. I hope you understood how you can utilize Facebook thumbnails effectively for promotion of your website.

Custom Pages

Once the Fanpage is created you can make your own custom pages. Unlike your Facebook profiles where you need to update everything on "Walls" on Fan page you have option of creating unique pages where you can notify people about your site. The unique pages are the custom pages which the new user can see when he will visit your fan page.

How to create custom pages?

There are 2 ways of creating custom pages.

- First is by using the iFrames where you use basic HTML tags for creating page which you like.

- Second is by using Facebook Mark-up Language (FBML) application where you use basic FBML tags for the creation of the page that you like.

Use of reveal tab

A reveal tab is nothing but an extract of custom page and is created in same way as that of custom pages that is by use of either FBML or iFrames. Its main aim is to restrict some custom pages so that restricted custom pages are accessible to only those visitors who is a "FAN" of that page which means who has liked the page.

Good Content is a key for good traffic:

It is obvious to get a good traffic for your website you need to have a "GOOD CONTENT" in your website. This is the mail reason for the visitors to visit your website.

In the same way in order to get likes for your Fan page you need to have a good content in your page with regular updates, links, videos, pictures etc. If by any chance visitor will not like your content he can easily unlike your page and never come back to your page ever. So you need to be very specific regarding "good content"

Contacts

Just like having a good content in your fan page is important, getting involved with the audience is also of the same importance. Getting involved with audience means you need to provide regular feedback to your readers, answer their questions in short and precise manner. This will not only help you to get the feedback for your content but can also help in the addition of new visitors. Answer the questions, run polls, ask questions. All these little things are really going to be helpful in future for increasing traffic.

(b) Twitter:

Twitter is considered to be famous social media for the promotion of your website. I myself am a big follower of twitter. Twitter is a great tool for getting a good traffic for your website and can also help you to widen your network of friends from all over the world. You can use twitter in a very productive way for your business. The most important feature of twitter is that the people are using it widely and you can easily find number of people who will be interested in your niche.

Following tips you can use to make your twitter account useful for increasing the traffic to your website.

Driving traffic to your blog or website from twitter:

Let me explain this through my point. I always try to update on twitter about my website or blog and gives all the updates regarding my website or blog on twitter. It feels so good when you tweet something about your website and the people starts re-tweeting it and hence spreading it to the world.

Using Website and Twitter Together:

Promoting twitter on your website can also be

very helpful and there are quite few ways with the help of which you can do this. The most obvious and common way of doing it is by displaying a "Twitter" button on your homepage or can also put within the sidebars so that it get displayed on all the website pages. With the help of this button people can directly go to the twitter site, sign up there and start "following" you. Displaying sharing links on your posts can also help in the promotion of the twitter from your site.

Another great way to promote Twitter on your site is to display sharing links on your posts. One more way of promotion of your website or blog is by displaying a "AddThis" button at the top of the blog or website. This will allow anyone reading your blog or website to share it in any of the social media including twitter also. Through this way you can count the number of new visitors liking your blog or website.

Promote Yourself:

You have to promote your blog and yourself very well in the twitter. If you will perform well in this it will prove to be very beneficial to you for the long run. When people will visit your twitter account the first thing that they will read in your twitter account will be your bio so be very specific while writing the bio of your twitter account. This may sound quite easy but trust me it's not. I personally would suggest you to spend some quality time on this as it going to be very effective for your website promotion.

One of the good way of promoting your website is by tweeting about it. Tweet about your website and keep people updated with your website. Amazingly many people think that tweeting again and again about your website will be considered as a spam. But it's not true! If you will tweet after every 5 minutes on a new post that can be categorized as spam. But the promotion of your website by tweeting about it again and again is not at all a "SPAM".

Create Friends:

Twitter is a social site so you have to be social. Keep in mind there are lot of people in there who are interested in your niche so you need to get involve with the people. Chat with them, try to give instant answers to their questions, you can also get involve with people by taking the initiative on your own and asking questions. This will help you in increasing your contacts all over the world.

Blogging is a community where you can find the blog of the people that is very much relevant to your blog you can have interaction with them and can also share idea.

Pay attention To Your Twitter Followers:

The greatest thing about twitter is that have instant reactions for your tweets from the followers. If you have tweet a particular post on the twitter and hardly any people has re-tweet it which means your followers are not interested in that particular post so it is important for you to listen to your followers as it can be helpful for you (to get traffic for your website) and for your follower too(to get the good information about the particular topic).

Honesty Is the Best Policy

This phrase is very important in every aspect of your life and business also. You should be very honest on the twitter. Being honest can always help you to reach the heights same is the case with twitter. Being honest on twitter can help in increasing the followers of your page.

Tweeting something which is not true won't help in raising your business for a long run!! If you will come up with something that you think your followers will like then tell your followers about it. If there is something that you didn't like then also tell your followers about it and discuss out things with them. You will see all the followers will not like it but they will respect your honest opinion.

Like honesty is must for a relationship to go long, it is must for business also to go long and reach heights.

Straight To the Point:

On twitter it is not possible to write the post that will exceed the limit of 140 characters. This means you need to tweet to make your point. The more you tweet the better it will be. You have to provide maximum information to your followers with minimum characters. You should give yourself time to think about your title so that your title should be short and snappy. Any link that you would like to include has to be short. This can be achieved with the help of many "ONLINE URL SHORTNER" websites. I myself use "bitly.com" to short all my links. This is a good tool that helps in reducing the amount of space which your links takes in the tweets.

Twitter- Background:

Twitter permits you to customize twitter account that is you can change the color of your account; your own background image can be uploaded.

How customization can be helpful?

With the help of customization you can make your account look different and unique from other accounts which will make you stand out from the rest of the crowd. The background image is the significant part of the process. You can portray a lot of useful information to your followers with the help of background image. You can display the address of your website, company logo or can also display the products (if you are promoting any) in your background image.

(c) Google Plus:

Google Plus has just been introduced in the world and millions of users have already signed up following more users day by day. So we can say Google Plus has a great demand. Now I have already discussed with you how Facebook and twitter helps you to drive traffic to your website. Is Google plus something different or the same that is sign up and start sharing or following the post.

I have discussed some ways that will help you to drive traffic to your website through Google plus.

Getting good rank in search engine:

One of the great things about blogging is to get good traffic for your website. Blogging is an awesome thing to rank your website high in search engine like Google. The majority of traffic for my blog comes from Google and I too concentrate to improve myself for SEO (Search Engine Optimization) of Google as it's famous among all the search engines.

One of my blog post started getting a good rank in Google search results after the installation of Google+ button on my post. It happened due to reason that some people has given me a few "+1" that helped a lot to be in the first page of Google results.Google+1 button has played a great role for improving Search Engine Results Page (SERP).Google +1 button has a great scope in future also as its tied up with the "GOOGLE" – a well-known search engine all over the world. And many people have already installed it and many more to come.

Boost Your Traffic

When you post one of the links of your articles on Google+ you will get a good   interaction from many people as Google+ has made it quite easy to interact with other people. You can refer any individual for a particular blog in the same way some people will be referring for your blog and hence increasing traffic to your blog or website in this way. Also you can leave a blog, comment or can simply click on "+1" button if u liked the particular blog.

I haven't use Google+ for long but still can see the results. For the short span that I used Google+ has helped a lot in increasing traffic for my blogs. The number of new visitors that I got from Google+ in such short span is, I guess, more than what I usually get from Facebook and twitter.

Awesome "Circles":

The best feature of Google Plus is its Circles. Circles permit you to add people within different sections. Circle helps you to keep "family" in one circle, "friends" in another and can have different circle for "work colleagues". In short Circles helps you to keep your contacts neat and in an organized manner. If there is a person who is your friend also and is your business partner also you can add him in both the circles.

Whenever you post anything on Google+ you will have the option of posting it under which section like within "friend" circle ,"family" circle etc.

For example I want to go out with my friends so I can post like "who's in for going out today" within "friend" circle and in the same way I can discuss my work related issues under "work colleague" circles. You can create as many circles as you want and can post things on it which means you can contact with many different groups through one profile.

You need not to create different Facebook page to communicate with people that like your site. Just make a circle for everyone that likes your site and communicate and share things with them through that.

Blogging

For promoting your websites online blogging is considered as one of the best ways for it. When you write a blog for your website it gives visitors a chance to keep coming back to your website to keep themselves up to date with your latest posts and hence they have to come to your website to read that particular post which will help in increasing the traffic for your website. It's not that easy as it seems you just not have to write the blog for your Website and it will increase the traffic for your website. You need to write a blog which is rich in content and also should have a unique content. While writing a blog for your website you need to very clear about the information that you have to convey to the readers.

Guest Blogging

You can also network with people who have blogs through guest blogging. You can find the people who write blogs through blogosphere. "Guest Bloggers" can blog on your blog. Usually a guest blogger will contact you and will ask to post a blog for his blog. In the similar way you can also ask the guest blogger to post a blog for your blog.

The benefits which you will get from guest blogging is discussed below:

Grow Your Audience – Guest blogging seems to be very helpful for the growth of audience as other bloggers are blogging on your blog which helps you to discuss about that particular blog and hence helps to increase contacts.

Increased Traffic – Guest Blogging is also helpful for increasing the traffic to your blog. You just need to make sure that you are posting your blogs on a blog which already has a good traffic. This will help to increase traffic for your blog as some traffic from there can get divert on you too if they find that particular topic interesting and want more information on that through your blog.

Increased Profits –Obviously when you have grown a good number of audience and a great traffic from guest blogging you are more likely to get increase in your profits too.

Article Marketing

If you are able to write your articles on your own you can put your article in many well-known article directory sites like Go Articles, Ezine, hub pages etc. This will also help in increasing traffic to your website by providing backlink from the content to your website. The person reading your article, if found interesting, can also visit your website. Article Based Backlink is typically considered as slower process compared to other backlinks.

Directories

Newbie Bloggers finds it quite difficult to understand how directory submission is helpful for SEO. Some new beginners are not even aware of directory submission.

So I am going to explain you directory submission from the very basics.

(a) Meaning of Web Directories

Internet users used to find the relevant information on web directories before the arrival of any search engine. Directories give appropriate information regarding any particular topic with great relevancy. But now we have best search engine like Google that helps to search anything quickly.

(b) Meaning of Directory Submission in SEO

Directory submission is a technique to put website or blog into web directories. It consists of putting your website URL with the details about site into most suitable categories

(c) How Directory Submission is helpful for SEO?

Directory submission is helpful in increasing the index of website by receiving backlinks from great web directories. Receiving backlink from great web directories will help in increasing the traffic to your website or blog and hence helps for a good page rank.

(d) How Directory Submission is done?

Directory submission is not at all a tough job. You just need to do the follow below steps:

- I have found a very helpful article while researching which is a goldmine of directory submission websites. Here's its link http://www.stephow.com/2014/01/top-100-high-pr-directory-submission.html

- All these sites are sorted according to their page ranks.

- You can click on any of the websites in the list and you will be directed to the directory website. For example Sitepromodirectory, Highrankdirectory, etc.

- Some of these websites require you to create an account or submit an article in order to register your website in their directory while some others allow you to register directly.

- You need to choose a relevant category for your blog or website according to the niche of your website.

- These categories are divided into various sub-categories, I recommend you to be as specific in your selection as possible.

- Once you come across the most suitable category related to your website or article that you are submitting, click on the Submit Your Sitelink button.

- Before you submit your site, you are required to fill a form specifying your website details. Once you submit this form, your website will be registered to the directory after the approval process.

You are done!

Forum Marketing

Find forum which is related to your site and start getting involve in that community. You should try to answer the questions of the people, ask for the advice, reply to the threads etc. In short get involved with the people anyhow with the topic related to you. This will help to build your contacts and will also help you to get involve with someone who is master in your particular niche.

Photo And Video Sharing

If you are using any images or photos for your site then you should share them on great photo sharing websites like Picasa, Flickr, Photo Bucket etc. his will make people from Picasa and other photo sharing websites to see those pictures and like it and hopefully can also follow the link of your site and thus increasing the traffic to your website.

In the same way if you have any videos for your

site you should upload it on famous video sharing websites like YouTube, Vimeo etc so that people will see the video and if they will like it can have access to your link.

Photo and video sharing are two tools which helps people to find your content in a different way.

Social Bookmarking

Most of the blog beginners who takes online tutorial for SEO plans do not get any idea about "social bookmarking" strategy. It is due to the fact that they feel it's just not worth to put links on every social bookmarking sites. I will explain you backlinking through social bookmarking then at the end if you find it useful for your site or blog you can follow this strategy.

Let me start with the basics.

(a) Meaning of Social Bookmarking

It is a technique to bookmark your favorite web pages online so that you can read it anytime and anywhere with the condition that you should be linked with the internet.

(b) Why Social Bookmarking Comes?

We do the bookmark to some web pages that we want to visit again after sometime without internet. But if for any reason which include browser crashing, software formatting or you are not before the computer where you have saved that particular bookmark happens then we will not be able to reach that bookmark. To avoid this "social bookmarking" comes. You can use these bookmarks to easily mark your page and can read it later but internet connection should be there.

(c) Is social bookmarking helpful for SEO?

The web pages that we bookmark at renowned social bookmarking site is considered as great backlink for search engine. Great backlink helps in getting a good traffic for your site or blog and hence results in good rank in SERP (Search Engine Result Page).That is the reason SEO professional do consider posting backlink in well known "social bookmarking" site.

(d) How Social Bookmarking is done?

Like the directories I am sending you the link for

social bookmarking sites also. You can find here the list of well known social bookmarking sites sorted according to their page ranks.

http://www.vmoptions.com/social-networking-list.php?sort=prdesc

- Click on any of the sites from the above link and you will be directed to that particular site.

- Create an account on that site or you can also login through your Facebook account.

- Now after the login process click on your username at the top right corner of the page you will be able to see the menu and under that menu click on "Add a page" button.

- After clicking on "Add a Page" button, the form will get display on the screen which you need to fill up that contains all the information of your webpage that you want to bookmark like web page address, tags, category etc.

- After filling all the information about your webpage click on "Add This Page" button and you are done..!!

Note:

Don't just start putting your links in social bookmarking sites after going through this tutorial. The submission of your link should be done in a proper manner so as to avoid any SEO penalty which can have a bad affect on blog ranking. Therefore there are many things to consider before submission of your link.

Local Listing

You might find listing in local directories more useful depending upon your site's niche. If you have a website that promotes your local business you can put it under the section local directory instead of submitting it globally and increasing your competition for no reason. This will help you to reach the targeted audience in a better way. You can submit your websites in sites like Yahoo local, Yellow Pages, Google Local etc.

Chapter 5:
Offpage Automation Tools

There are many types of Offpage automation tools which are:

Majestic-SEO, BuzzStream Link Building, SEOmoz Linkscape, Raven SEO Tools, SoloSEO Link Building Tools, Yahoo! Site Explorer, Page Inlink Analyzer, HubSpot Website Grader, Link Diagnosis, Advanced Link Manager.

Some of the Offpage automation tools are explained below in detail:

Seomoz Linkscape:

SEOmoz is a tool that helps in tracking inbound link. It is available in both the versions i.e. basic version as well as advanced version.

Basic version: It helps in determining the number of inbound links that can be linked to your page and can also give us information about the number of domains that can be related to your page. The tool also gives us the rank of the page depending upon the number of quality "inbound links" linked with the page. The rank of the page also depends upon the rank of the domain linked with the page.

Advanced version:
In advanced or full version you cannot only get the number of "inbound links" and the number of domain linked to your page but can also get this information of your competitor also which helps you to compete with your competitor.

Advantages:

- Free (paid options are also available for getting more inbound links and domains)
- Analysis of anchor text is available.
- Quick and simple
- This tool allows you to compare with other sites.

Disadvantages:

- You cannot do analysis beyond 1000 links for free.Payment is required.
- It cannot help you in tracking the link-building progress.

Majestic Seo:

It permits you to track the link information of their own sites as well as of their competitors. If you will register yourself with Majestic SEO the service for your site will become free. You can also buy credit to get the information about your competitors.With this tool you can access

- Pages
- Images
- "NoFollow" links
- Sub-domain
  Advantages:
- Free (paid options are also available with more functionality)
- It helps you in comparison with other sites.
- It separates .edu and .gov links which allows quick analysis for quality links.
  Disadvantages:
- Do not have sophisticated interface.
- Require payment or subscription for analysis beyond 1000 links.

Senuke

The Senuke has many features. The most appreciable among that is it allows submission of website to over 2000 article directories, social bookmarking sites, forums, Wikis and Web 2.0 sites and the awesome part is that you can also submit to Wordpress blogs. Register for a bunch of free accounts which has free hosting sites after that install Wordpress and then use Senuke which will automatically post your content to an infinite number of self hosted Wordpress blogs.

Advantages:
- User friendly
- With the help of "Turbo Wizard" you can literally get quality of links which will be just a button away.

Advanced Link Manager

This tool doesn't only helps in link analysis but also promotes the ability of automate link building which includes configure to source websites get the details of their contact and starts sending request to those websites automatically.

Advantages

- Avaliability for the analysis of "Anchor Text"
- Quick
- It can also help in tracking link-building progress.

Disadvantages

- The cheapest version of this tool costs you around $99
- You need to download the software of this tool. It can't be accessed directly through web browser.

DISCLAIMER AND/OR LEGAL NOTICES:

Every effort has been made to accurately represent this book and it's potential. Results vary with every individual, and your results may or may not be different from those depicted. No promises, guarantees or warranties, whether stated or implied, have been made that you will produce any specific result from this book. Your efforts are individual and unique, and may vary from those shown. Your success depends on your efforts, background and motivation.

The material in this publication is provided for educational and informational purposes only and is not intended as medical advice. The information contained in this book should not be used to diagnose or treat any illness, metabolic disorder, disease or health problem. Always consult your physician or health care provider before beginning any nutrition or exercise program. Use of the programs, advice, and information contained in this book is at the sole choice and risk of the reader.

www.ingramcontent.com/pod-product-compliance
Lightning Source LLC
Chambersburg PA
CBHW071010180526
45168CB00003B/1365